MY LIFE IN THEIR HANDS

by Stephen Gallagher
with Julie McKiernan

This book is dedicated to John 'Chops' Chasty who made me laugh, bought me a pint and made me feel like an able-bodied person.

Introduction

I've been trying to get this book written for at least five years. After watching the film *My Left Foot* based on the autobiography of Christy Brown, the author and poet who lived with cerebral palsy, I realised that, despite being born thirty years apart, we have faced similar prejudices. People still assume that if you're disabled and can't speak you must have a learning disability. So I decided it was time for a new book about what life is really like for non-verbal disabled people. Several volunteers offered to help me write it but we rarely got beyond basic biographical information. So, in 2018, I asked my social worker to find someone more experienced to work with me.

She contacted Healthy Arts, a not-for-profit arts and health organisation based in Wigan who suggested their writer, Julie McKiernan. We started by creating a timeline of my life, then Julie began to ask me questions to fill in the gaps. Lots and lots of questions! She had to learn not to ask more than one at a time and to give me chance to reply; while I had to learn how to type longer answers than a simple 'brilliant'. My support workers called Julie my 'book lady'. For an hour every Monday morning she would come and make notes then go away to type them up, ready for us to read through and edit the following week. She interviewed my parents, my sister and an old schoolteacher. She even arranged a reunion of some of my old Scouting friends. She would stop at nothing to uncover the truth.

But the man who knows me best is me, so I always got the last word.

I want this book to explore and explode some of the most common myths about people with disabilities, and I want to surprise each and every one of you with what goes on in my head.

Most importantly, I want to thank my amazing mum and dad who have made me the man I am today; my lovely sister, Julie, who has always looked out for me; my old pal Dave and all my other fantastic Scouting friends who opened up the world for me; and all the support workers who have looked after me with so much care and kindness over the years.

CONTENTS

Chapter One

Myth 1: All disabled people are born that way.

Chapter Two

Myth 2: All disabled people get the help they need.

Chapter Three

Myth 3: All disabled people have learning difficulties.

Chapter Four

Myth 4: Disabled people don't like to take risks or be ridiculed.

Chapter Five

Myth 5: Disabled people can be cured by prayer.

Chapter Six

Myth 6: Disabled people who can't speak can't think, learn or have an opinion.

Chapter Seven

Myth 7: All disabled people like doing the same as other disabled people.

Chapter Eight

Myth 8: Disabled people don't fall in love.

Chapter Nine

Myth 9: Able-bodied people have it easy.

Chapter Ten

Myth 10: Disabled people don't have hopes, dreams and ambitions.

Acknowledgements

Chapter One

Myth 1: All disabled people are born that way.

Not all people are born equal and, to some people's surprise I suspect, not all disabled people are actually born disabled.

When I was delivered at the Christopher Home in Wigan, Lancashire, in June 1962, fourteen months after my sister Julie, my parents, Tommy and Joan Gallagher, were delighted to have a son and felt their family was now complete. My dad returned to his job as an insulation engineer working around the north west of England. My mum, who had left her factory job, became a typical 1960s housewife and mother to two young children. We lived in Beech Hill, an area to the north of Wigan town centre. Mum would push us up and down the hilly streets in our big Silver Cross pram to do her shopping and other errands. Her parents lived nearby in Springfield and my Dad's were round the corner in Beech Grove. We were an ordinary family in an ordinary northern town until, when I was six months old, I caught an ordinary childhood complaint, gastroenteritis. Most children suffer for around three days with severe diarrhoea and vomiting then make a complete recovery. Unfortunately, I was one of the rare and unlucky ones who went on to develop viral encephalitis, an uncommon but serious condition in which the brain becomes inflamed or swollen. I was admitted as an emergency case to Whelley Hospital where consultant paediatrician Dr R.M. 'Sam' Forrester explained to my anxious parents that

I had inflammation on my brain and he was sending me immediately to Pendlebury Children's Hospital in Salford.

My parents were devastated. Not only was I unconscious and seriously ill but now I was miles away from home and they didn't have a car or a telephone. They had to catch one bus into Wigan town centre then another to Salford and the same to come home again; an exhausting four-hour round trip. My dad took unpaid leave for the first six weeks I was in hospital but, when it became clear that my condition wasn't going to change any time soon, he reluctantly went back to work. There was little financial support available back then, and they had to buy food as well as bus tickets, so poor Mum would make the long journey on her own, leaving my sister Julie with our grandparents. There was a public phone box four hundred yards from our house and my mum kept trekking down there at all hours of the day and night to check on my progress.

Then, one awful day, the police came to tell her I was dying. I was being fed intravenously, but after the nurses had used a vein once it would collapse and couldn't be used again, so they had got to the stage where there were no more veins left to try. One officer went for the woman next door to sit with Mum while another tried to get hold of my dad who was working in Southport at the time. Someone from his office finally managed to get through to him and said, "You've got to get over to Pendlebury straight away. I'm afraid your son's very ill." So a workmate put him onto the back of his motorbike and rushed him straight there, in his work clothes, with no helmet. In the meantime, the police blue-lighted my mum and her dad to the hospital. When they arrived, they were met by a surgeon, Mr Dawson, who said, "We've exhausted Stephen's body. Surgery is now the only option. There's a clot on his brain and what I'm going to try to do is very dangerous, but if I don't do something he'll die. Do I have your permission?" Of course, my parents had no choice, "If it saves his life, yes!" But then they had to sit and wait an agonisingly long time to see if I survived. Apparently, Grandad Jim was little help as he kept crying all the time and repeating, "I can't believe this. There is no God." At least looking after him must have been a distraction.

During the surgery, Mr Dawson went in one side of my forehead and out the other. I still have the scars. It was weeks before he told my parents exactly what had happened. "I got in and I could see the clot so I got a straw, an ordinary drinking straw, and I put it near the clot and started to blow." His colleague, who was assisting, was watching my face and cried, "Keep going! I can see something." Apparently, my facial expression was gradually changing as I became more responsive, so Mr Dawson kept blowing and, encouraged by his assistant, managed to lift the clot high enough to remove it from my brain.

My distressed parents were relieved that I survived the operation and couldn't thank Mr Dawson enough, but he warned them, "Stephen is going to be damaged and we can't tell you how badly. Only time will tell." Once they had seen me, and wept at the sight of my heavily bandaged head, my exhausted parents were finally persuaded to go home to rest. When my mum rang the hospital later to check on my progress, the nurses reported, "Stephen's smiling at us. He's watching us, following us round with his head." However, it was to be a long process of recovery and I was kept at Pendlebury Children's Hospital for almost a year. At first, I had to be turned every fifteen minutes, so when my mum and dad used to visit and take me out in my pram, they'd walk the three miles to Walkden and back, stopping regularly to gently rotate me. Needless to say, they were desperate to take me home, but when the doctors finally said they could and my mum exclaimed, "Thank God," they warned her again, "Now your trouble really starts, love."

Chapter Two

Myth 2: All disabled people get the help they need.

My sister, Julie, must have been surprised when I finally did return home. She'd seen me being taken away in an ambulance and every time she heard the ice cream van chimes after that she used to think it was the ambulance bringing me back and went looking for me. Well, that was her excuse anyway. Her first instinct was to climb into the pram with me like she used to do, but obviously she'd grown in my absence so had to settle for stealing my dummy instead. One of the first gestures I ever used was sucking my thumb to represent Julie.

Actually, I'm surprised she recognised me when I finally did come home as I'd lost so much weight and my left side had been affected by the surgery, particularly my foot. It kept turning round so a surgeon had to come out to our house and show Mum how to put a plaster cast on it every night. No-one knew what the future would hold for me. The only certainty was that I would never walk and would need a wheelchair, so my parents decided to move house. My dad was at work seven days a week, and it was clear my mum wouldn't be able to carry me upstairs to the toilet or bathe me on her own for much longer. So Dad went for a look around a new estate of bungalows that were being built not far from our semi-detached house. He came back with surprising news: he'd reserved the only one with a level driveway. Most people plan to move to a bungalow when they retire but my parents were still young. They had to look years ahead to ensure they would be able to care for me as well, and for as long, as they possibly could.

It's incredible now to think they had no help with any of this but, in the unenlightened 1960s, families were expected to get on with things and no-one seemed to care or even understand how they felt. Except for Dr Forrester. He was Wigan's top paediatrician for many years and much loved for the great work he did for children in the area. A local reporter remembers him as 'a true gentleman dressed in a brown cord jacket… making everyone feel at ease.' Dr Forrester suggested that parents like mine form a committee to address the lack of local facilities for children with physical disabilities. This resulted in the Wigan and District Spastics Society being formed in 1965. Dr Forrester said, "I can help in one way only and that is to give you the names of people who have handicapped children," which, of course, he wouldn't be able to do today because of data protection. But he said, "There are so many people that I've looked up and they're just sat at home. There's nothing happening for them at all." I was fortunate that my mum was able to take me out every day but some parents couldn't, or simply didn't want to, because of the stigma attached to having a disabled child. So Mum and Dad rounded up a couple more parents and they went knocking on doors. Sadly, some people wouldn't even admit they'd got disabled children. "There's nothing wrong with my child," they insisted, and there was nothing my parents could do but walk away. But they were determined to bring together people who were facing the same problems, to share their experiences and support one another.

So when Poolstock Cricket Club offered the Wigan and District Spastics Society committee use of a ramshackle old shed where the teams used to change and shower, the committee put out an appeal to anyone who had a physically or mentally disabled child or adult. Parents could leave their children there for two or three hours and committee members like my mum and dad would look after them while the parents did some shopping or had a bit of a breather. Obviously, they couldn't keep this going for long as they each had responsibilities of their own, but it was enough time to get to know other parents and what their children needed. And it gave them the ammunition to kick-start a campaign to demand suitable local schools and nurseries for children with physical disabilities. In the meantime, my mum, desperate to find more stimulation for me, enrolled me at Rodney House nursery school in Longsight, Manchester. She took me there and back every day by bus, but it was a disheartening experience as the staff regularly told her, "Don't get your hopes up. He won't be able to do anything."

Fortunately, Dr Forrester didn't agree with this diagnosis. One day, on a regular home visit to see me, he told my parents, "Stephen has more intelligence than you realise. Those eyes tell a story. Please don't let anybody tell you different." My mum says she always knew that I understood everything. A mother's instinct, perhaps, or simply because she spent so much time with me. She told Dr Forrester,

"If you say anything to him his face lights up. If something's wrong, he'll tell you. I can tell what he wants by knowing all his signs." I started making simple physical gestures from early on and, fortunately for me, my parents quickly cottoned on to what I was up to. As a family, we were soon able to communicate on a basic level. But, one day, my determination to communicate helped to prevent a very nasty accident. A young couple came to live next door and my mum and her new neighbour, Eva, got on well. They were always in each other's houses, especially after Eva had baby Deborah. One day Mum nipped next door and, of course, took me with her. Eva was in the kitchen so Mum left me alone in the living room with the baby who, by then, was crawling. All of a sudden, Mum and Eva heard a terrible noise. It was me knocking like hell on the foot-plate of my wheelchair! So they ran into the living room and found Deborah crawling towards the electric fire.

Despite my own disabilities, I think I always had an instinctive desire to protect others, much like my sister Julie. When she was at Sacred Heart Primary School, one of the boys who had seen her with me at church or perhaps the school gates, came up and started to mimic me by making funny signs and noises. Her teacher later told my parents, "He's the cock of the school and everybody's frightened of him, but Julie jumped on him and knocked hell out of him. I would have stopped them if he'd been hurting her but, as he wasn't, I let the other children watch and he was shamed to death afterwards."

Chapter Three

Myth 3: All disabled people have learning difficulties.

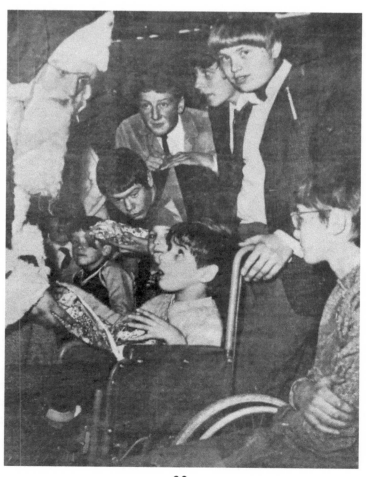

I decided several years ago that I wanted to write my story so that people would know what it feels like to have a disability and to have people make so many assumptions about you; for example, that because you're in a wheelchair you won't notice you're being served a lousy meal. All my life people have seen my chair and not the person in it. My family, friends and support workers all see 'me', but there are still times when I feel discriminated against. I was recently in a book shop with my mum and the woman behind the counter refused to serve me because I was in a wheelchair. Presumably, she thought I didn't have the intellect to choose my own book.

People often assume I have a learning disability. I get that a lot.

Thankfully, my parents took Dr Forrester's advice and tried their best to stimulate and understand me, but even they were surprised to discover that I had taught myself to read. I was four or five years old and watching *Pogles' Wood* on children's television with my mum one day when I decided I wanted to watch *Trumpton* on the other side instead. So I pointed to the programme listings in the TV magazine then to the telly to show my mum I wanted her to change channels. When my dad came home he found her sobbing next to me on the settee and, thinking something terrible had happened, exclaimed, "What's the matter?" Mum stopped crying long enough to gasp, "He can read!" Needless to say, my dad didn't believe her. "What are you talking about? Don't be silly," he said. "I'm telling you," Mum insisted, "He can read." And she explained what had happened. My dad was amazed. "Not only can he read - he can tell the bloody time and all!"

When they'd both finished crying, they sat and thought, 'Where on earth do we go from here?' It was all very well discovering that I could read but, at the time, there was little in the way of special school education and they were ordinary people dealing with an extraordinary situation. It is to their credit that they just got on with looking after me and dealt with every problem as it came up. They are amazing parents. They have been there for me every step of the way and nothing has ever been too much trouble for them. Even now, in their eighties and nineties, they are still looking out for me.

Fortunately, they had help from Dr Forrester who was instrumental in setting up Mere Oaks Special School in Standish. He formed a committee which included the Wigan Infirmary physiotherapist, other medical staff, and, of course, my mum and dad. They raised money to build the school through regular street collections, standing outside big Wigan shops like Woolworths to rattle their collecting tins. They were such familiar fixtures that once, when my dad was stood outside Marks and Spencers waiting for me and my mum to come out, someone pressed some shillings into his hand!

Although the committee was organised and took great care with the finances, when it came to actually buying land and finding an architect and builder, they handed everything over to Wigan Council. Mere Oaks Special School opened in September 1968 when I was six, the name being chosen by Dr Forrester. I can vividly remember my first day there, because I sat in a paint tray with all my new clothes on.

The Headteacher was Mr Marshall. My parents thought he was brilliant because, if you had a problem, he'd come to your house and talk to you. I thought he was caring and clever. He saw potential in me that others didn't, but he could also be a strict disciplinarian. Back then, in the 1960s and 1970s, corporal punishment was an accepted part of daily school life, but it may surprise you to learn that it was also applied to disabled children. One day, when I was fifteen, I got caught smoking in the toilets. My friend, Peter, had brought a pack to school and, along with another friend, we decided to give smoking a go. I guess I just wanted to be like everyone else but I can't say that I enjoyed it. It was my coughing and spluttering that gave us away. Mr Marshall caught us and hauled us off to his office where he gave each of us a ticking off then used a pump across our backsides. It seems strange now to think that such an adult activity received such a childish punishment. Even at the time, it seemed unfair, and I'd hate to see corporal punishment come back in schools. Mr Marshall also told our parents. My dad said, "If you ever do it again I'll tan your hide." Neither he nor my mum ever smoked - and I haven't since.

I took to school immediately but, in the early days, I used to bite my hand in anger and frustration when people couldn't understand what I wanted. Fortunately, I had a great teacher in Miss McVitie. She noticed that I was always looking at and paying attention to what was going on around me. She had been on a course for teaching handicapped children, in London, and had moved up from Bedfordshire to come and work at the school. She says she found communicating with most of the children a problem at first due to the broad Wigan accent, but I was a special case. So she talked about me to a parent of one of her friends, a scientist who was interested in machines, and he came up with an idea. "It was a board with short sentences and pictures on it and, if you worked with simple questions,

Stephen could answer. Even if it was simply 'yes' or 'no', he could do it himself and we knew that he understood." Miss McVitie had further proof of this a few months later when I went home very excited one afternoon and took my mum to the cupboard where she kept the biscuits. I pointed at the digestives then mimed cradling a baby. Miss McVitie, whose nickname was 'Biscuit', had married a Mr Lang a few months earlier and I'd obviously noticed an important change in her.

The new Mrs Lang, and the rest of our teachers, were pioneers in the early days of special needs education and had to make the curriculum up as they went along. They believed in active teaching and encouraged us to try all kinds of activities no matter how much of a mess we made of ourselves and the classroom. Mrs Lang had been a PE teacher before she retrained, so she disguised physiotherapy as a gym class to make it more fun. "I used to take them into the gymnasium and we'd prop the forms up against the bars so that there was a slight slope. The children loved to pull themselves up then slide back down again."

Following the success of my communication board, Mrs Lang encouraged me to use Makaton, a unique language programme that uses symbols, signs and speech to enable people to communicate. But I was always looking for new and more effective ways to communicate. In 1976 when I was fourteen, one of the young girls who worked in the office, Diane Brogan, was walking around the school in her dinner hour and stopped to say hello to me. I watched her go back to the office and get on her typewriter. A couple of days later when she came round again, I pointed and made noises until she cried in frustration, "Oh I don't know what you mean, Stephen." She went to find Mrs Lang who watched and listened then said, "Stephen wants to go in your office and have a go on your typewriter." Diane let me and this came to the attention of Mr Marshall who asked my mum and dad if I could help the school to get a new Possum typewriter. Possum is Latin for 'I can' and was adopted as the brand name for the Patient Operated Selector Mechanism or POSM in the early 1960s. He said, "We need this not just now for Stephen, but for other children like him who will come to the school in the future."

The problem was that the Possum cost around £9,000 and the school had to prove it was going to make a difference to my life. So an important doctor came from Yorkshire to do tests on me at Pendlebury Children's Hospital. He asked my parents, "How do you know what he knows?" And my mum replied indignantly, "I just know that he does!" The doctor got a tray out and he put all these little objects on it and I thought, 'What the heck's he doing here?' Then I realised that he wanted me to connect them up, so I pointed to the cow and then to the moon and then in the air, and he burst out laughing and said, "You're right, lad. Hey Diddle Diddle the Cat and the Fiddle!"

As a result of the good report he wrote about me, I was given the opportunity to try out the Possum typewriter in a room full of local councillors and dignitaries. I was asked to type something. When I hit each key it flashed up the letter then printed the full word off at the end. Suddenly, someone important and slightly pompous said, "How do we know that you, Mr Marshall, have not prearranged and rehearsed this?" And he demanded that I type something spontaneous. So I typed "Have a look in my mouth." The man looked and saw that I had an empty tooth socket. I typed again. When the paper came out, Mr Marshall ripped it off and showed it to everyone. They all started laughing. "My dad came home from work last night and pulled it out." Dad admitted that he'd extracted the tooth with pliers because he was afraid I'd swallow it. It was lucky he did as it was the proof they needed to get the school the Possum typewriter; and further proof that I could and did understand what was going on around me. Finally, I could communicate through words as well as signs.

Chapter Four

Myth 4: Disabled people don't like to take risks or be ridiculed.

When I was about thirty, a large group of my friends and I went to Haydock Park Races for a mate's stag do. I'd only ever gambled on the Grand National before but I placed a bet just to join in. And lost. It's safe to say that I'm not a risk taker with money but, despite my disabilities, I do like to take risks in life.

I think my teacher at Mere Oaks, Mrs Lang, recognised this quality in me and that's why she encouraged me to join the Cubs. She was a Cub Scout leader herself so she knew the types of challenges and opportunities the organisation could offer. With my parents' consent, she checked out local groups on my behalf. Unfortunately, the group at my own church, Sacred Heart RC, was inaccessible as the building had too many steps; but the nearby St Andrew's C of E (12th Wigan) Scouts' hut only had three steps which were more manageable. There were nerves and concerns on both sides as the group had never had a disabled member before, and my parents were worried about my being accepted by the other Cubs and being able to physically cope with the activities. My mum was particularly worried that they wouldn't be able to understand me, but some actions transcend language and, during that first Christmas, when I fell face first into a jelly we all laughed together. As Mrs Lang said, "Stephen took to Cubs like a fish to water," so, unlike some of my classmates who joined but left after a while, it seemed natural for me to progress into the 12th Wigan Scouts when I turned eleven.

I was the first Scout in the troop to use a wheelchair - in fact the only one during my whole time there - but the leaders, Alan 'Skip' Davenport, Kevin Foy and Dave Thomas, were magnificent in the way they encouraged and enabled me to join in all the activities. They put me into Eagle patrol with Gareth Humphries, now an MBE, as my patrol leader. He quickly told the youngest patrol member, Brian Heeley, "You can look after him." I knew Brian from Cubs but, as he later confessed, "Because Stephen had physical disabilities I assumed he had learning difficulties as well. The first thing I remember is trying to teach him to salute. We got some wine gums and every time he got it right he got one. But at the end of every Scout meeting his dad would come over and ask him what he'd been doing and I'd be trying to tell him but he'd be listening to Stephen, and I remember asking, "How do you know what he's saying?" Gradually, I realised he understood what was going on, so I started to talk to him and got rudimentary responses back. I knew if he shook his head he meant 'no' and if he gave me a black look it meant, 'What are you doing that for?!'

At Cubs, our Akela, Sandra, dealt with my personal care, but at Scouts the leaders decided it was everyone's responsibility. As Gareth remembers, "If Stephen wanted to go to the toilet he pointed and one of the lads used to take him. They'd take his pants down, sit him on the toilet, close the door and shout, 'Let me know when you're finished.' Then Stephen would kick the door and they'd go in and pull his britches up. No messing. It was just part of growing up." But Brian, being Brian, made it fun to get round the embarrassment; in other words, he teased me rotten. As I hit puberty, I grew a lot of body hair or, as Brian said, "He was basically covered in fur so I used to make quips about werewolves. He was the first person with disabilities that I'd got to know. I could never imagine the difficulties that Stephen faced but I thought the best thing to do was not to take it seriously. If there was something he was having problems with we'd make a joke of it. We understood that it was serious but it wasn't a conversation that we wanted. We wanted any interactions to be fun." I really appreciated that and the way the other Scouts treated me.

Fellow Scout, John Barnes says, "We involved him in everything, treated him like anybody else. No more, no less, that was it and that's how he developed." They took me everywhere with them from sporting events and presentations to sailing on Scotsman's Flash and, although I couldn't camp overnight, my dad regularly took me to spend the day with them at Bispham Hall, the Scouts Association activity centre in Billinge. They also pushed my chair up and down countless tracks around the Lake District and taught me to abseil at Brownstone quarry near Bolton. I had to wear a safety harness and be strapped to one of my mates, but it was brilliant. Considering I'm usually so close to the ground in my chair, I was surprisingly okay with heights and it was great finally to be able to look down on the world instead of seeing everything from knee height. Unfortunately, I never got the chance to try potholing but I'm not afraid of going underground or being around water.

Most people only have to rely on themselves and the equipment they use, but I have to rely on other people, too. I've always had to put my life in other people's hands and this has made me, by necessity, a very trusting person. My parents were always determined I should make the best of my life and I think some of that has rubbed off on me. This is why, when I was sixteen, my Scout leaders nominated me for the Cornwell Scout Badge, the highest award for bravery in Scouting.

I was stunned, but thrilled, when the District Commissioner for Wigan Scout Council, Mr. T.E.B. Parkinson MBE, wrote to tell my parents that the Chief Scout, Sir William Gladstone, had awarded me the Cornwell Scout Badge. Mr Parkinson said, "We are all very proud of him and conscious of the tremendous example which he has set for us all." He added that I was the first Scout in Wigan ever to receive the award. "So you have made history for Scouting in Wigan. The Award is some recognition of your own pluck and determination and bravery, and is a great credit to your Parents and to the Scouts and Leaders of the 12th Wigan (St. Andrew's) Scout Group." I was glad that he mentioned my parents and gave them the credit they fully deserved.

Over the next few weeks we received several letters, but one stands out from Wigan's Director of Education, Mr R.C. Hopkinson, who wrote to congratulate me but also addressed my parents "to show appreciation for all that you have done for Stephen... behind this award were two devoted parents who had given hours of encouragement and patient understanding".

Unfortunately, on the day I was due to be presented with the Award by the Queen at Windsor Castle, I developed chicken pox, so the ceremony had to be postponed. I finally received it from Sir William Gladstone himself, who travelled all the way up to Wigan from London. The Wigan Observer covered the story and, as far as I know, my photograph is still somewhere in the Scouts' archives. My certificate states 'in recognition of his high standard of character and devotion to duty under great suffering'. My wheelchair foot-plate certainly suffered as I broke it when I stood up to accept the award!

Not long after the award presentation, I moved up to Venture Scouts with Brian, and Dave Eastham, both of whom I'm still in touch with. They could already communicate with me on a basic level but getting my first communicator was to make a world of difference to our friendships and to the way the other Venture Scouts interacted with me. Basically, they treated me like anybody else which meant they relentlessly took the mick out of me!

When they asked if it was okay to take me to Tyldesley baths to try kayaking, Mum said,

"Of course you can, but don't get his feet wet."
At the time, taking someone like me canoeing
was unheard of. There was no hoist so they had
to pick me up between them and thrust me into
the canoe. Despite being unable to swim, I
managed a full 360 degree roll. Not through
choice, though. Gareth Humphries MBE
recalls, "We put him in the canoe and put a
spray deck on him, and he paddled around as
best he could. Then we said, 'Right, now you
have to learn how to capsize,' and we took
hold of the canoe and turned him over. I can
still see his face as he came up spluttering!"

My face was equally expressive when they
took me to Alton Towers and insisted that I try
The Nemesis. It was one of those rides where
your feet dangle down, so Brian quickly made
an important decision, "Stephen has the feet of

Houdini. I've never known anybody who can get out of shoes like he can. No matter how tight you tied them, ten minutes later there'd be one flying across the room because he'd got excited about something. So I thought we'd better take them off because they wouldn't last the ride. Stephen nearly didn't, either. For some reason, he didn't like it. When we got back to the start, the lad came over and said, 'Do you want to go round again?' Stephen shook his head. But it had been hard work lifting him on and off all the rides all day, and I was enjoying sitting down, so I said, 'Yeah, he wants to go round again.' The lad was looking dubiously at Stephen who was vigorously shaking his head, so I said, 'Don't worry about that, it's his condition. His body does the opposite to what he wants. He's nodding on the inside.' Stephen was giving me the blackest look, but we went round again!"

I accidentally got my own back one St George's Day parade when Brian was pushing my chair towards Wigan town centre. We were coming down the hill at Bridgman Terrace and there were people stood along both sides of the road. Suddenly, I saw someone I recognised so I decided to stop and say hello. Unfortunately, Brian was also looking around and he didn't notice me putting my brakes on... "The wheelchair he had then was slightly shorter than his current one," Brian remembers, "And the handle was at a crucial height! So I was doubled over in agony in the middle of the street, in front of all these people, and he's just waving, couldn't give a sod!" So, later that year when the Venture Scouts took part in the

St Andrew's walking day parade, we were coming down Baytree Road, which is proper steep, and I saw my mum and dad so I started waving. As soon as I'd got my hands in the air Brian let go of my chair and I took off! I'd freewheeled a few yards, scrabbling to reach the brakes, when, to my relief, somebody managed to get in front of me and catch me. I turned back to Brian and gave him a filthy look to signify, "Why?!" And he grinned, "Remember St George's Day?"

I loved the way Brian and the others treated me like any other Venture Scout. As Gareth said, "We had no sympathy for anyone!" But he added, "It helped the young people to grow. They were dealing with stuff they'd never seen before. It made them sit back and think differently. All the girls used to spend time with him." Ah yes, the girls. Our unit often met up with Ranger Guides, and even other units who had female Venture Scouts, so I got the chance to get to know girls and they gave me lots of attention. As fellow Venture Scout, Eddy Worthington noted, "I'm surprised they didn't wear his knee out with sitting on it!" Socialising was a big part of Venture Scouts and I was always included in trips to the pub after meetings. Eddy again, "We were always in a pub. That was fundamental to everything we used to do, really. Tommy used to tell us not to get Stephen too drunk, but one night in the Bricklayers we got carried away. We put him on whisky so he wouldn't have to get his dad up in the night, but he ended up legless."

I should have left Venture Scouts when I turned twenty-one but, after they celebrated my birthday with a phallic stick of rock and a photograph of me as 'Sergeant Wooff', I was allowed to stay on until the unit disbanded in 2000. That was a sad day for everyone but for me in particular as I knew they were all going on to new adventures while I was just losing a lot of great friends. Some did stay in touch, like Dave, and Brian who still takes me to a local beer festival every year. But I didn't realise at the time what an impact I'd had on them. I'll let Brian sum it up, "A lot of people don't know anyone with a disability as disabling as Stephen's, but all the Scouts and Venture Scouts that met him saw the way the rest of us interacted with him and so they did the same. There was a ripple effect. It got them over the stigma and the fear and they got to know Stephen as a person and treated him like anyone else. You didn't see the wheelchair, you just saw Stephen."

Chapter Five

Myth 5: Disabled people can be cured by prayer.

Sometimes I feel like I am a burden to my family and think that I have had enough, not of living, but of being stuck in this chair. So whenever I am feeling low, or even just a bit fed up, I think about how lucky I am compared to others. There's always someone worse off than you, like a good mate of mine who has to be fed directly into his stomach via a tube, bypassing his mouth ('peg-fed') and can only use his eyes to communicate. When I was in the Scouts, it definitely helped to be surrounded by boys who could physically do more than me as it spurred me on; but things have changed as I have got older. I can't just live in the moment anymore, and time has made me more aware of all the differences between my friends' lives and mine. The feeling of 'Why me?' has got more regular as I have got older.

I used to believe in God, and sometimes I'd still like to, but, if there is a god, I'd like to ask him or her, 'Why am I stuck in this chair?' I don't believe in life after death so, if this is the only life I'm going to have, why would God be so cruel?

Like my parents and sister, I was brought up Catholic. Our local priest at Sacred Heart RC Church in Springfield, Wigan, was Canon Gerard Walsh. He regularly used to see Mum there on a Sunday but when he asked my dad, "Do you come to church?" Dad replied, "Occasionally, yes". Canon Walsh said, "I never see you." So Dad explained, "I'm usually at the back where there's more room for Stephen's wheelchair." "Come to the front row", Canon Walsh said. "I want to see him." As my verbal communication has always been limited to sounds, rather than words, my dad was worried I might make unintentionally funny noises and make people laugh, which would be disruptive as well as disrespectful. But Canon Walsh insisted, "If you don't come to church, that's fine. But if you're coming I want Stephen on the front row." This proved useful on one occasion when the canon was coming down the steps from the sacraments and his hanky fell out of his sleeve. I kept pointing to his nose and then the floor until he realised what I meant and genuflected gracefully to pick the handkerchief up. So I was surprised when he didn't respond to my enthusiastic waving at the opening of Liverpool's Catholic Cathedral in 1967. He was taking part in the ceremony as one of the Canons of the Cathedral Chapter so the whole family went to watch but, of course, he couldn't acknowledge us because he was on the telly.

He was like a father figure to me. I looked up to him. At a time when, like much of society, the church could be very patronising towards disabled people, I felt like he was really trying to see beyond my chair and reach the person within it. He came to give me religious instruction but he also used to talk to me about football. He was a Liverpool fan and that was a massive influence on my becoming one, too. My mum used to confide in him her worries about me, but he told her to focus more on my sister, Julie. "It's her you want to worry about," he said.

When I was seven, my mum wanted to take me to France, to Lourdes where the spring water is believed to be responsible for many miracles. Dad was sceptical but said, "I suppose it can't do any harm". I'm not sure my sister would agree. At only eight years old, she found the whole trip a bit scary. It was our first time on a plane and the passengers were all singing the prayer *Ave Maria*, which didn't exactly fill us with confidence, especially when we were already nervous. Poor Julie was travel sick on the way there and, when we arrived, she was faced with the distressing sight of lots of sick people being carried around on stretchers. My mum confessed that when we went in the water she really did hope a miracle would happen. It didn't, but an amazing coincidence did; as she was trying to explain to one of the nuns that she was English, the nun said, "It's all right. I understand. I come from the Convent of Notre Dame in Wigan."

I was only young so I didn't really understand what the trip was about but, when I was older, a local woman came to see my parents and offered to take me as part of a group from St Mary's and St John's churches. It was funded by HCPT, a charity that offers supported pilgrimage holidays to Lourdes. I only really went to make my mum happy, but it was a free holiday and most of the volunteers were young and female. When we arrived I asked if I could ring home and, suddenly realising that my parents were so far away, I broke my heart down the phone.

I don't know if it was because of that experience but I stopped going to church when I was about twenty-one. It was hard for me to stop going, because I was living at home at the time. My dad was okay about it, but my mum went mad. She probably thought bad things would happen to me. Like things could be any worse.

Chapter Six

Myth 6: Disabled people who can't speak can't think, learn or have an opinion.

Being unable to speak is one of the most frustrating aspects of my disability because it limits my communication and, as a result, many people assume that I don't actually have anything to say. They talk over me, or even in front of me, assuming that I won't understand. For many years, I was unable to share my thoughts or needs with anyone beyond my close family, friends and support workers, and, even then, I was restricted to what I could convey through simple gestures and sounds. So the happiest moment in my life was when I got my first Canon Communicator in 1978, shortly after leaving school. The Canon was a portable tape typewriter. The keyboard had the alphabet, numbers and other symbols. Each roll of tape was very long and could hold about 12,500 characters. It was a big turning point for me because, unlike the Possum typewriter, it was portable and attached to my wheelchair so I could type words wherever I went and print them off on ticker tape. Finally I had a 'voice'. It was brilliant!

The Canon Communicator was presented, on behalf of the Variety Club of Great Britain, by actress Violet Carsons who played Ena Sharples in my favourite soap opera, *Coronation Street*. I'm not ashamed to say that when she gave it to me I cried because it meant so much. It took a bit of getting used to at first as I don't have the most dexterous of fingers, so the first words I typed were short and simple: "Hi Dad". But practice makes perfect and I was soon proficient enough to hold full conversations. Brian Heeley remembers, "When Stephen got the Cornwell Badge, it was the first time he turned up with the communicator. To be honest, I still get emotional thinking about it today because I was absolutely gob-smacked. I think we were all taken aback. After all that time, to actually have a proper conversation, it was humbling really." When we used to go for a drink after Venture Scouts and my dad came to collect me, there would be ticker tape all over the floor. He'd pick bits up, read them and go, "Whoa! Better not let your mum read this, Son." The communicator changed people's perceptions of me very quickly. For instance, there was a little girl in our street who was afraid of my wheelchair and the fact that I couldn't talk. But one day, when she asked me something, I typed out an answer and she took the ticker tape, pushed it down her sock and went home. She came back every day after that to talk to me and is now married to my mate, Paul.

All the way through my years at Mere Oaks my parents had been thinking ahead and worrying about what would happen to me after I left school, but now the communicator meant we could discuss what I wanted to do next. They were surprised when I told them I wanted to go to The National Star College, a specialist further education college for people with disabilities at Ullenwood Manor near Cheltenham in the Cotswolds. My physiotherapist at Mere Oaks School, Lesley Wrightson, used to work there and she suggested that I apply. It would give me a chance to study at a further level and give me greater independence as I would be a residential student. I was particularly interested in their two-year course on the History of Art which I'd been obsessed with ever since I'd seen a TV documentary about Salvador Dali.

At first, my parents were upset that I wanted to leave home and go away to college, particularly as I was only sixteen, but typically they decided if that was what I wanted, they'd make sure it would happen. My dad said, "I don't care how far it is. If he wants to go, he can go." However, this proved to be more complicated than expected as first I had to go to Fitzroy Square in London for an assessment. My parents and I stopped in a big house belonging to the Spastics Society, and I sat awake all night looking through the window, too nervous to sleep. The examiners had received a report from Mere Oaks but they wanted to test my understanding themselves. Fortunately, I passed their test. Then I had to have an interview with The National Star College's Principal, Mr Field, who said, "Yes, we'll take Stephen, but you'll have to apply to Wigan Council to pay his fees." So it was a relief when, in November 1978, my dad finally received a letter informing him that the Education Committee had agreed to pay both my fees and my travelling expenses.

Travelling wasn't as easy as expected, either. On the day I was due to start, there was a tanker drivers' strike. My dad couldn't get enough petrol to drive there and back so we had to go on the train. In those days, the trains were made up of small compartments with no room for a wheelchair, so we had to travel in the goods van with some racing pigeons, a couple of greyhounds and a rottweiler. It was snowing when we finally arrived, and I broke my heart when my parents had to leave me to get the train back home. They were very upset too and, as they later admitted, expected me to be on the phone the next day asking to come home. I actually settled in quickly. My sister said the house was quiet without me. I'm not sure if that was meant as a compliment or an insult.

I soon met other students and went on to have a great social life. There were regular activities outside lessons, including going to the local pub. I remember getting drunk for the first time on whisky and lager. It felt brilliant until the next day when I woke up with a hangover and found myself in trouble with Mr Field. But I didn't want to waste this opportunity and soon learned to knuckle down and get on with the work.

We looked at the whole history of art and went on regular trips to galleries to study famous paintings such as Turner's enormous seascapes which I loved for their scale. We were actually down in London in 1979 when MP Airey Neave was killed by an IRA car bomb outside the House of Commons; but we knew nothing about it until we got back to college in sleepy Ullenwood that night and saw the evening news.

We had regular written exams which meant the college had to employ a scribe to write my answers down for me. However, I was encouraged to use my hands to propel my own wheelchair about. This was a bit of a shock as I was used to being pushed around by my parents and friends, but it was a bigger one for my parents when they came to visit and saw the state of my hands. It was clear I couldn't cope so, in my second year, I was given an electric wheelchair. This, along with moving into a room in a shared house on the campus, made me feel much more independent: until one day when the damned chair got stuck in mud!

Unfortunately, I had to leave the chair behind when I left college, so going home felt even more like a backward step, especially when I discovered that the qualification I'd gained wasn't recognised in the 'normal' able-bodied world. I'd enjoyed the course but, once

I left the college's protective bubble, I felt even more aware of being a second-class citizen. And that made me both angry and sad.

But I was determined to keep on learning new skills and prove what I was capable of. So when my parents and I heard about Fourways Assessment Unit, a service for adults with disabilities run by Wigan Council Social Services, I was keen to give it a try. I moved into the building in Cleworth Hall Lane, Tyldesley, in 1981 and, as my movement and flexibility were deteriorating, I was given another electric wheelchair, this time for keeps. It gave me greater independence but it wasn't without its problems. One day, it malfunctioned and drove me straight into my own TV! My Venture Scout mates thought this was hysterical and teased me about it every time they came to collect me. Between them, they had drawn up a rota to pick me up and take me back every week so that I wouldn't miss a meeting.

Unfortunately, like a lot of provision for the physically disabled, Fourways was only meant to be short-term so, after two years of activities, events and outings, I found myself faced with returning home and staring at four walls. It felt like I was being thrown back out onto the street and my dad was not happy, especially as we weren't made aware of any other local provision. But he'd heard about Oaklands, a Leonard Cheshire home in Garstang, which offered supported living with regular activities. I decided to give it a try and thought it was okay at first, but I soon noticed that a lot of the residents were much older than me and most of them were in bed by eight o'clock. I'd been there for two weeks when the accident happened. I went to use the lift and the doors opened but, unbeknownst to me, the elevator floor hadn't fully aligned with the lobby floor so when I moved forward my chair tipped backwards. I was stuck there for what seemed like ages until a young carer came across me and called for help. It took several people to lift me out as the chair was so heavy. I'd hit my head and my eye brow needed stitches but, thankfully, I wasn't knocked out. I stayed on for a couple of weeks after that, but I didn't feel safe anymore and I knew my parents were worried. So I moved back home and started to attend Larch Avenue Day Centre in Pemberton. I remember my first day there vividly because I was still in bed when the transport came to collect me.

2001 was a big year for me as it was the year I finally moved out of the family home, at the age of thirty-nine. It's a long-standing joke between me and my dad that I should have asked Jeremy Kyle to find out if Julie is my real sister as she left home so much earlier than me! I was very happy living with my parents, but I wanted to give them a break from being my carers. They were both getting older and I knew they were struggling even though they would never admit it. So I felt sad but excited when I got the opportunity to move into a supported living bungalow. Julie remembers crying when she first heard the news and wondering how I would cope, especially being so far away from my mum and dad.

I hadn't been there very long when The Sequal Trust, a communication disability charity, came to ask if I needed anything and offered to buy my second communicator. This was a real turning point in my life because, finally, I literally had a voice. It was incredible and that's an understatement. It was a 'light writer', a switch and keyboard communication device that enabled me to type messages which were then relayed through speakers by an automated voice. I was presented with it the day before my birthday. The lady who ran the charity said, "We'll get a celebrity to present Stephen with it." Naturally, I asked for a Liverpool player, but they were away in Europe at the time, so they rang Manchester United who sent Paul Scholes. Julie's partner, John, thought this was hilarious but, to be honest, I didn't care who gave it me as long as I got it. What was funny was that it spoke my words in an American accent. My mum and dad couldn't stop laughing when I typed 'Asda' and it said, "*H-asda H-asda*" like John Wayne!

When I used the light writer in public, people would stop and stare because they could see that I wasn't talking but they couldn't make out where the voice was coming from. My parents remember being in a queue to pay for a book when suddenly they heard, "Dad! Dad! I want to go the toilet. I'm brasting!" Mum was mortified when everyone turned round. Dad also remembers a time we went to Bolton Market, "We were next to a French stall and Stephen started playing *La Marseillaise* on his machine. We were all wondering where it was coming from. There's devilment in him." So you may not be surprised to learn that I do actually use my communicator to swear. Not in front of my parents, but I have been known to use the F word with my mates. After all the typing, I changed from being left-handed to being right-handed virtually overnight because my shoulder was aching. It was only then I realised I am ambidextrous. My third communicator was supplied in 2012 by Embrace, a local charity that works towards a better life for people with disabilities and their families.

Chapter Seven

Myth 7: All disabled people like doing the same things.

Being disabled sometimes feels like you are part of another race with its own separate and distinct culture. People are often surprised, disappointed, or even angry, when you don't want to conform to the services offered or dare to demand something different. Day care provision has improved enormously over the years that I have used it, but I am surprised it is still so segregated. Although I am well looked after and enjoy the company of my fellow service-users, it doesn't feel right that we are all grouped together just because we are disabled. Not everyone with a disability wants the same things in life. This may be the only thing that we actually have in common.

Over the years, I have attended Fourways Assessment Centre, Larch Avenue Day Centre, Fabrex Adult Training Centre and Hunter Lodge Day Centre. All of them are, or were, similar in their approach. We took part in regular activities, many of them arts and crafts based, engaged in some sports (I could play pool with assistance) and went on a wide range of outings. Although I met new people, I also regularly found myself reunited with old friends from school as we all moved in circles around the same institutions. When people ask me what I've done over the years it isn't always easy to remember as the days blur into one another. It irritates me when I hear people moaning about their jobs as I think, 'At least you can do one!' I can't tell you how frustrating it is never to have known what it's like to get up in the morning with a sense of purpose, or to feel the satisfaction of a job well done. My dream job would be a TV quiz host but, failing that, I think I would have liked to have been a teacher or even a support worker. The latter may surprise you but I really do admire them. I have had to depend on others for my intimate care all my life but no-one has ever made me feel uncomfortable. Wiping other people's bottoms takes guts because you have to deal with the other person's embarrassment without revealing your own. I like support workers to be straight-talking, and a good sense of humour can really help, along with a lot of patience.

I, too, need a lot of patience on a daily basis to explain to people what I want, especially with those who don't know me well and aren't familiar with my short-cut gestures or sounds. Although the communicators have obviously been a big help, it can be laborious typing out letters and words, particularly if I am tired, so it's great when I can do things for myself. I've loved reading ever since my mum used to buy me Ladybird books from Wigan Market. Unlike a lot of people who stop reading when they leave school, I continued because I enjoy it so much, and because it is something I can do with the minimum of help. It's really satisfying when I can go into a bookshop and browse and choose my own books simply by pointing at them. This may seem like a small thing to some people but it's a massive deal to me and very empowering. That's why I regularly ask for book tokens for birthday and Christmas presents. Once I get my nose into a book, I can read all night. It takes me out of my chair and into the wider world. When I read I forget who I am and immerse myself in the characters. I particularly enjoy fast action thrillers with lots of tension. But I also enjoy biographies and autobiographies because I'm nosy and curious about other people's lives.

Television is another great window onto the world and is something else I do have some control over. I have my own TV in my bedroom and can use my Possum keypad to select the programmes I want to watch. Like many people in the North West, I grew up watching *Coronation Street* because it was set in our local area and featured people and events we could recognise and relate to. It has, of course, changed over time, but I find the modern story lines more exciting. My dad did some work as an insulation engineer at Granada TV so I got to go and visit the old *Coronation Street* set twice. It was a lot smaller than it appears on TV but that didn't destroy the illusion; in fact, it made it seem even more real when I watched it afterwards.

My all-time favourite TV viewing is quiz shows. As I mentioned before, people often assume that, because I'm in a wheelchair and can't speak, I don't have an intellect, but watching quiz shows has always been a bit of a thing in our family and something my mum, dad and I still like to do together. I particularly like quizzes which are more intellectual in tone as I like to watch clever individuals exercise their brain power and pit their wits against the questions. I also like trying to guess the answers before they do.

While I'm able to exercise my brain, I'll never be able to exercise my body. Seeing so many disabled people now taking part in sports is inspiring, but it can also be a bit disheartening and even upsetting for those of us who will never be able to join in. Instead, I have to settle for watching sport from the sidelines or on TV. My dad first took me to watch Wigan Warriors Rugby League team play at Central Park in Wigan when I was nine or ten years old. I love watching rugby league because the controlled aggression makes it so exciting and the players use the whole of their bodies rather than just their legs. I like how, when they go for a try, it's almost like watching them fly. I follow Wigan Athletic Football Club because of the usual family allegiance passed down from parent to child, but my dad also follows Manchester City so wasn't impressed when I started to support Liverpool FC under Canon Walsh's influence. However, travelling regularly to Liverpool is too difficult, or at least that's what my dad says, so I have to settle for watching their games on TV.

Although it's sometimes annoying to watch other people move their bodies so freely when I can't, I do enjoy watching snooker, darts and athletics. I have quite a methodical mind and a strong sense of order so I particularly enjoy the way that in snooker they work their way round the table via the different ball colours. I also find the rhythmic click of the cue and the soft thud of the balls against the cushions very soothing. Snooker, like darts, is full of showmanship and big personalities which I guess is the case in athletics, too. People might assume that because I'm a wheelchair-user I would naturally want to watch the Paralympics but I rarely do. I prefer to watch able-bodied athletes compete because they are generally faster and stronger. I would prefer to see disabled athletes compete against able-bodied athletes rather than against one another; the Paralympics can seem a bit patronising at times, as though the competitors are being looked down upon. I have never taken part in any athletics myself, unless you count an egg and spoon race - which I lost!

I've found a lot of comfort in music over the years. I have quite an eclectic collection of CDs ranging from rock music to - well, William (Bill) Tarmey who played Jack Duckworth in *Coronation Street*. I was at

Granada Studios when they recorded his *This Is Your Life* episode on Thursday 22nd October 1992. I was the decoy. He thought he was going to present me with a communicator, but instead I let Michael Aspel into The Rovers Return. I made a brief appearance at the start of the show, and my mum, dad and I got to stay to watch it being filmed. It was the first time I'd met Bill Tarmey, or heard him sing, but I bought his CD afterwards. There are two songs that mean a lot to me: *Wind Beneath My Wings* and *IOU*. Both of them make me cry, especially the line 'I would be nothing without you' which always reminds me of my dad. *IOU* is my favourite song as it really gets hold of me when I am down and lifts me up. I also love country music, probably because there was no escaping it when I lived with my parents as my dad listened religiously to the Sunday afternoon Joe Fish Country Show on BBC Radio Lancashire. I like the way the lyrics tell a story and make you want to know how it ends.

In complete contrast, my favourite band is *The Who*. I know they've been around for a very long time but I only really became aware of them seven or eight years ago at a neighbour's eightieth birthday party. Technically, that's not true as we got the date wrong, so it wasn't actually his birthday, or a party, when we showed up. Nevertheless, his daughter put a record of *My Generation* on. It was the first time I'd ever heard it and I loved the lyrics, not because I 'hope I die before I get old' but because the anger, aggression and rebellious nature of the song summed up how I feel about being stuck in a wheelchair and constantly underestimated by people. It's difficult to listen to rock music in shared accommodation without headphones, but I can't put them on so I can't listen to any of my CDs without assistance. If the support workers are not busy, they're always willing to help but sometimes I just get tired of asking.

I never get tired of eating. I'm lucky in that I've never had to watch my weight. My sister says I was the envy of the family when I was growing up because, although I never stopped scoffing, my stomach stayed flat. When I was younger, before I got my first communicator and could only use a limited range of signs and sounds, it was difficult to tell my parents which meals I didn't like so I just used to shove them away. But now, every morning, my support workers ask me what I want for my tea. If I asked for pie and chips every day they might advise me to choose something different but generally they are happy to cook whatever I want which, being a typical Wiganer, is traditional northern food like meat and two veg. However, I have become a bit more adventurous over the years and have tried mild curries, chilli and Chinese food. Fortunately, I can hold a fork and feed myself with solid food if someone cuts it up first, but it can be a slow process so I've had to get used to cold food.

I also enjoy going out for meals, but it isn't always easy to eat in public when you have a disability. Once, on an assisted holiday in Blackpool, we went into *Harry Ramsden's* chip shop. The staff and the food were great but, as we were sat there minding our own business, a man came over and snarled, "They shouldn't let disabled people in here, putting us off our food." I felt like nobody. I was angry, too. The support workers didn't say anything at the time. I think they were too shocked. The other diners didn't say anything either, but the staff confronted the man. He swore and started to get aggressive so they told him to leave. When we got back to the hotel, I asked the reception staff to phone the police. They came to interview me and returned the next day with the news that they had traced the man from my description and CCTV, and had arrested him for a hate crime. Luckily, that's been my only really unpleasant experience, but I am used to attracting unwelcome stares from fellow diners who seem to find me more fascinating than their food. Julie shares my frustration, "It takes patience when you go to a crowded restaurant, and no matter what you do in advance, like ringing up to say one of the guests will be in a wheelchair, you end up being furniture removers when you get there."

Generally, I have a healthy appetite. I always say, "If you will cook it, I'll eat it". I once had a go at cooking myself. What a disaster! I tried to cook an omelette at Hunter Lodge and nearly set the kitchen on fire.

Chapter Eight

Myth 8: Disabled people don't fall in love.

I am sure that if I wasn't disabled I would be married by now. Of course, I realise that being able-bodied isn't a guarantee you will meet someone, but I'm also pretty certain that being disabled has held me back. So, as the years have passed, seeing so many of my able-bodied mates getting married has only made me more aware of the differences between us and made me feel increasingly angry and sad about what I don't have. This feeling has deepened as I have grown older because I worry that I will spend the rest of my life alone. Don't get me wrong, my family is wonderful but I had hoped that I might have had one of my own by now.

When I was younger, I thought that meeting the right person was just a matter of time so I did everything I could to make it happen. I even grew a moustache because, in the 1970s, American actors Burt Reynolds and Tom Selleck, as well as all my mates, had one. My dad used to shave me but, at sixteen, I asked him to leave my top lip alone. I was tempted to grow a beard too, but he said I wouldn't suit one and I believed him. These days, only one of my mates still has a moustache but it feels a bit late to shave mine off now. Besides, my top lip would feel naked.

In the 70s, I grew my hair longer which wasn't just a fashion choice, it was also a bit of a rebellion against going to get it cut. Today, the mobile hairdresser comes and styles my hair in the privacy of my own home but back then my dad had to take me to the local barber. This was a problem as the door was too small to fit my wheelchair through so my dad had to leave it outside and carry me in. This was as humiliating as it sounds, even though the barber was brilliant and tried to make me feel as comfortable as possible.

What I wear has always been important to me. Just because I'm a wheelchair-user it doesn't mean I don't want to look as good as I can. I try to go for a casual but smart look. My support workers take me shopping and have a pretty good idea of what I like by now. But when I lived at home my mum used to help me buy my clothes. Dad would drop us off in Wigan town centre and we'd go round the shops. But being honest, no young man should ever have to go shopping with their mother. It made me feel self-conscious and embarrassed, as though everyone was looking at me. Mum had quite good taste, but sometimes I'd indicate something I liked and she'd give her honest opinion and suggest an alternative which, being more suitable for my dad, I'd politely refuse. Sadly, practicality has always had to be my key concern. My clothes need to be easy to get on and off, and they need to be comfortable enough to sit around in a wheelchair all day; so no tight waistbands. This was particularly frustrating when I was a teenager as I longed to wear jeans like all my friends or tight high-waisted flares like Roger Daltrey of *The Who*. I did have some flares, and at least I couldn't make myself look even more ridiculous by strutting around in them!

Roger Daltrey never seemed to have any problems attracting the interest and attention of women and, to be fair, neither did I. Unfortunately, it was the wrong kind of attention. I've never struggled to find women willing to look after my personal needs - to push my wheelchair, feed me or keep me company but I don't want pity and sympathy. Sadly, I seem to have the same good taste as lots of other men as, although I have met plenty of women I have been attracted to, they have always been spoken for. It's a joke between me and my mates that the only thing I'm ever likely to pull is a muscle. I'm okay with the jokes. I'm used to them by now. They don't upset me because I know they'd all be made up if I ever did meet someone. The problem is where. Going to the same day centre every day means that I usually only come into contact with the same people, some of whom I have known for years. I spend the rest of my time with family, friends or support workers so I don't have much opportunity to meet new people and even online dating is difficult due to my disabilities. I suppose I could get a friend to help me create a profile and choose a date but, really, would you want someone to do that for you?

I did recently enjoy the chance to go on a date night arranged specifically for people with physical disabilities. Not surprisingly, it was organised and run by a lady who used to work at Hunter Lodge and understood the frustrations and desires of those she worked with. I suppose it's a sign of progress that she was even able to arrange such an event, as it's not too long ago that it was frowned upon for people with disabilities to date, let alone marry and have children. The event was held at a local social club, and it was brilliant. I 'spoke' to five different women for fifteen minutes each. Not all of them had a disability. They were all able to speak and I used my communicator so we were able to 'chat'. Inevitably, some of the conversation revolved around disability with questions such as, "What's it like being in a chair?" prompting my own response of, "Would you go out with someone in one?" Then we all had to mark one another out of ten, and we got told our own scores at the end. The highest mark I received from the women was nine and my lowest was four. The highest mark I gave was eight and the lowest was two. Sorry, but she was a bit boring. Fortunately, the person I gave eight to was also the one who gave me nine. I am still waiting for a rematch! There was no follow-up directly afterwards, but we did exchange numbers. I tried to ring her but it went straight to answer machine and, although I left a message, she never called me back. I like to tell myself that she accidentally gave me the wrong number or her answer machine wasn't working. Either way, I live in hope there will be other similar events in the future.

I first fell in love when I went to college. One of my fellow students, Laura, made it very clear from the start that she fancied me and I fancied her like mad, too. She was tall with dark hair. She had multiple sclerosis. To make meal times run smoother, and to stop our food getting cold, some students used to help others with their food. Laura volunteered to feed me which gave us plenty of opportunities to get to know each other better. But it was still a surprise when she suddenly declared that she loved me in the middle of the dining room! I was shocked, but chuffed to bits, especially when she followed up with a big warm hug. She waited until bedtime to make her next move. Let's just say that she put me to bed that night. The college was fine about relationships between students and we were inseparable for the rest of the course. My parents met her when they came to see me and tried their best to help us stay in touch after we left college. But she lived in South Wales and phone calls were no substitute for being together. Gradually, we drifted apart. I would love to see her again and hear what she has been up to in the intervening years.

I found it hard to move on after Laura, not that there were many opportunities to do so. I'm not being vain but I think I'm a decent enough looking bloke, and I have received my fair share of compliments over the years, but I'm only expected to fall for disabled women, as though it's a crime or ridiculous to fancy an able-bodied woman. Perhaps, then, this isn't a good time to reveal my crush on Sally Dynevor (Sally Metcalfe) from *Coronation Street*! I have only been in love once since Laura, with a fellow service-user from Hunter Lodge. I was even going to propose, but she finished with me because I chose to spend Christmas with my mum and dad instead of her. She's now going out with my mate and, looking back, it was my biggest mistake.

I once asked my dad if he thought I'd have made a good father and he said yes. I would have liked to have children and raise them like he did us. He's the best dad ever and my best mate. Like many men, I would also have liked my name and bloodline to carry on. I know that my disability was the result of an infection and that, in all probability, if I hadn't had that infection, I would have remained able-bodied. Had my condition been genetic, I wouldn't have wanted kids because I would have been frightened of passing it on. Knowing the life I have had, I wouldn't wish this disability on anyone.

It is very hard to think that my parents won't always be around. That's why I want to settle down with someone before they do pass away. So they don't have to worry about leaving me on my own. Unfortunately, the chances of that happening are like Wigan Athletic winning the Premiership. Mind you, they said that about Leicester City, didn't they?

Chapter Nine

Myth 9: Able-bodied people have it easy.

Most people would look at me and assume that my life is difficult and, to a certain extent, they would be right. It has been hard to make myself understood over the years and I have had days when I have felt low in mood but, apart from my disabilities, until recently I've enjoyed pretty good health. My family members are the ones who have had it tough and I can't thank them enough for the way they have looked after me and fought for change on my behalf.

I've been blessed with very special parents and, like many disabled people, I have a closer relationship with them than most people do with theirs because I've had to rely on them my whole life. They both did so much for me, fighting hard to get the right support and opportunities.

My dad turned ninety-one last year. He grew up in a large family in Wigan so it was a case of 'first up, best dressed' and I think that made him more determined to achieve what he wanted in life. He's my best friend and I think we are very alike. We're both patient but stubborn and find it hard to hide our emotions. My sister, Julie, remembers that when we were kids and we went to the shops in the car, I'd burst into tears if my dad went inside. She would have to reassure me, "He's coming back. He'll only be a minute." Dad's always been very protective of me and determined that I should be involved in everything; at Christmas the family would play cards for tuppences, or board games like *Snakes and Ladders*, and he used to play on my behalf.

He was an insulation engineer and had to work really long hours to keep the family afloat. He's always been a very fit, strong man and thought nothing of lifting and carrying me everywhere. Now I've got an adapted car, he doesn't have to lift me in and out anymore but he still takes me out regularly and to hospital appointments. If we go for a meal, he will always insist on feeding me first, even if it means that his meal will be cold by the time he gets to it. He doesn't care how long it takes me to chew, as long as I eat.

My decision to move out of the family home caused a lot of upset at the time. My dad was seventy-ish and he wanted to see me settled. He didn't know, obviously, at that time how long he had got left and how much longer he could carry on lifting and carrying me. He and my mum wanted to know that I would be well cared for and they found it very hard to let go. At first, they even wanted to continue to buy my food when really they just needed to accept that nobody else could look after me the same as them.

We're coming to the point now where my dad is struggling to do some of the things that he once took for granted, and he will push himself to the limit. My sister worries there will be an accident but Dad has always said, "If I died holding Stephen, I'd die happy." Though I suppose that's not much good if he cracks my head on the floor in the process!

As far as vices are concerned, I'm my dad's only one. My sister says I'm his drug of choice. He has let looking after me dominate his life and, in a way, that's probably kept him going, though his own dad, Grandad Gallagher, did live to be ninety-two. When I was still at nursery, my dad was involved in a bad motorbike accident. He needed skin grafts so my mum, Joan, had to travel all the way to Preston to see him in hospital, as well as look after me and my sister. And all this without a car as she has never learned to drive. My dad was off work for a year but they still had to pay the mortgage. Mum was only in her twenties and must have wondered what on earth she had done to deserve so much bad luck.

Mum was born in Wigan, the only child of Irish Catholic parents and had a happy childhood. When she met and married my dad, she had a good job with chances of promotion. She planned to return to work after having children, but everything changed when I got ill. I was the first person in my family to be disabled. My grandparents were from a different era when people with disabilities either didn't survive or were hidden away so, at first, they struggled with having a disabled grandchild. But my mum's mother was regularly called upon to deliver babies and lay out the dead so she was the first one to rally round and offer help. Unfortunately, soon after, she was diagnosed with cancer so my poor mum had to do all Grandma's washing, ironing and shopping as well as doing her own and seeing to us. It must have been very hard dealing with all this at a time when most of her friends would still have been single and out enjoying themselves. It's not surprising that she suffered some ill health herself as a result but, incredibly, she just battled on.

When I started school, Mum looked for part-time jobs, like distributing leaflets and serving school dinners, which she could fit around the school day. When something needed sorting, like getting the council to agree to fund my education, my dad would usually deal with it, not because my mum was too quiet and shy - hell, no - but she was too busy being my main carer. She has always been lovely with me and gives the best hugs.

I first became aware of my sister when she stole my dummy. Being only a year apart, we used to share a pram with Julie perched on a little seat inside. But one of her earliest memories is of me being ill and the ambulance coming. She was frightened by the noise and by not knowing what was going on, and that was pretty much the pattern for the next few years. I don't think anyone really thought about what it must have been like for her as a small child with so much focus on me at the time, and she has only told me recently how she felt.

She remembers being three or four years old when she was taken to a place with lots of people in wheelchairs with illnesses that she found distressing and upsetting. "I remember going once and I was looking forward to seeing this beautiful little girl that I'd met the previous year, but she'd died. It was very hard to take in as a small child that other children are not as lucky as you and, as much as Stephen could annoy and irritate me at times, and vice versa I'm sure, I wanted to be reassured that he wouldn't die young as well."

A more common concern was how she and other people reacted to me being in a wheelchair, "There'd be children playing games in the street and Stephen would just be sat there watching me and all the other kids enjoying ourselves. When I was ten or eleven, I got my first proper bike and it suddenly hit me that Stephen would never do that." She was the only child at school with a disabled sibling and kids can be very cruel, especially when faced with something out of the ordinary that they don't understand.

Like my parents, Julie soon learned to understand what I wanted, but getting the Canon Communicator really did change our relationship. Before then, whenever it was her birthday, my mum and dad would sign a card 'from Stephen with love' but now I could type out personalised messages. It was brilliant to finally have a conversation with her and things changed massively after that. She noticed me more and would offer to feed me to give my mum a break. That doesn't mean she found me any less annoying. When we were younger, she complained that when we went out people would stop and give me money. Clearly they didn't know what else to do when faced with a disabled child who couldn't speak or walk, but poor Julie didn't understand this at the time and wanted to know why they didn't give her any. "When I was growing up people would say, 'You must be neglected because your brother takes up all your parents' time' which was true to a degree but my needs simply weren't as great as Stephen's. I could go and get myself a bowl of cornflakes or make myself a slice of toast. But sometimes I did feel left out. Once when I got a cold I remember my dad coming to sit with me, and I thought, 'Well, I might be ill but at least now I'll get some attention'."

It made me sad to hear Julie say this because I was totally unaware of how she felt at the time. The problem was it was hard to tell what was 'normal' when our family life was so extraordinary, but she must have noticed the difference whenever she went to her friends' homes. Fortunately, she had one family member who was able to spend time with her on her own. After Grandma died, Julie spent a lot of time with Grandad Jim who lived five minutes' walk from her school. She used to have dinner with him every day and he would tell her stories about the old days. My sign for him was 'red nose'. He was disabled by a stroke in his eighties and lost his voice which gave him a greater understanding of my condition and we became close. When I broke my left big toe and my mum came to visit me at the hospital, I signalled to her that he had died. Goodness knows how I knew, but it was true. At eighty-three, he lived long enough to see me make progress, which was good as he and my dad's mum always worried that my parents were being too optimistic about my future.

As we got older, Julie's frustration would sometimes become apparent. She used to complain about my choice of TV programmes and tell me off for getting worked up and making so much noise that she missed the plot. Or she would argue with my mum because she wanted to go out on a Saturday with her friends instead of helping with the shopping. She just wanted to be doing what everybody else did which included bringing boyfriends home. "Of course I used to worry that they would head for the hills thinking there could be trouble or hard work ahead but fortunately it didn't pan out that way." Being disabled didn't stop me feeling like a protective brother and I thought no-one would be good enough for my sister until she brought John home. We shook hands and he talked to me like he would anybody else. I liked him straight away and nicknamed him 'Chops' because he had big cheeks. In return, he called me 'Gally' as an abbreviation of 'Gallagher'. He and Julie were together for over twenty years and, during that time, John and I would go for a pint and he'd make me laugh and encourage me to be daft. He also loved to embarrass me, like on my fortieth birthday when he surprised me with a Strip-o-Gram! So it was the saddest day of my life when, completely out of the blue, he died of a massive heart attack at the age of only sixty-four.

Chapter Ten

Myth 10: Disabled people don't have hopes, dreams and ambitions.

My favourite subject at school was geography. I loved learning about different countries around the world and their cultures and traditions. I would love to travel more but it isn't easy when you're in a wheelchair and need so much support. So far, I've only been to Lourdes and, once, to Ibiza in Spain. Fourways Assessment Centre arranged a group holiday and my mum and her friends came along to help out. We flew from Manchester and the stewards and stewardesses were brilliant, taking really good care of us just like the staff at the San Remo hotel. Most of the time we just relaxed and enjoyed the sun but in those days hotels were more formal and we had to dress for dinner every night. Mum was keen that I should look my best and the Germans at the next table kept saying how fine I looked which, of course, I lapped up. But I wasn't quite so keen on all the Spaniards slapping my mum's legs in her miniskirt!

We always holidayed as a family in England, and even that wasn't always easy. I remember once when I was little we went to Newquay in Cornwall. My dad's old Ford Escort wasn't good enough to get us there so we hired a purple Ford Marina, but even then we still had to stop overnight at Cheddar Gorge. There were very few disabled facilities or access so my dad constantly had to lift me in and out of my wheelchair. Fortunately, I was very light back then. But my parents went to all that effort only for it to rain all week. The final insult was when a pigeon got stuck in my mum's beehive! Perhaps that's why most of our holidays after that were spent back up north in Blackpool.

My dream holiday would be Disneyland in Florida or, failing that, its smaller version in Paris. I would love to see all the characters and locations from my favourite childhood films. Those films were great company for me when I was growing up and helped me to escape my chair through my imagination. Studying art had a similar effect because I could escape into the paintings. When I was at the Star Centre, we went to the Ashmolean Museum of Art in Oxford, and I fell in love with the city, its atmosphere of education and culture, and all its university colleges, museums and galleries. It feels like my spiritual home. I would move there tomorrow if I could, but all the bikes would be a pain as it's hard to get out of their way in a wheelchair.

Most people have no idea how difficult life can be as a wheelchair-user, until they have an accident or grow older and lose their mobility. That's when they discover how inaccessible many buildings and forms of transport still are. The Equality Act 2010 says 'reasonable' changes or adjustments should be made to ensure access, but some people can be very unreasonable and seem determined to make life difficult for others. I have seen a lot of positive changes in my lifetime but there is still too much discrimination against disabled people. I hope one day that all new buildings will be fully accessible. Let's face it, even ordinary homes should be built with larger-sized doorways because you never know what the future holds or who might visit. And don't even get me started on transport!

Stephen Hawking, Professor of Mathematics at Cambridge University, author of *A Brief History of Time*, and famous wheelchair-user, dramatically changed public perceptions of people with disabilities, but we still need better representation on TV and in films. We particularly need to see more disabled actors playing disabled characters. I think it's also very important for disabled people to vote, but to encourage them to do this we need more MPs with disabilities in the Houses of Parliament; although, if we're being honest, many of the current ones seem intellectually challenged.

I hope that you have found my book interesting. It has been amazing to finally have a chance to 'speak' through it. I hope family and friends have learned something new about me and that those of you who don't know me have been surprised. I hope I have challenged your perception of non-verbal people. We're all a bit quick to judge others on first meeting, myself included, but I hope this book encourages you to dig a bit deeper, look a bit harder and have a bit more patience when faced with someone different from and less articulate than you. When I look at other people's disabilities I think, 'My God, how lucky I am'. I don't want you to feel sorry for me, not a chance. Maybe my book will help me to achieve another dream which is to go on TV and be interviewed by Graham Norton.

Failing that, I'd be happy to get a light writer with a proper Wigan accent!

No-one knows what's around the corner in life. It's difficult for anybody, but I know I will always be looked after one way or another, and while my family is around they'll make sure that everything's okay.

Acknowledgements

Thanks to my dad, Tommy Gallagher, my mum, Joan Gallagher, and my sister, Julie Gallagher, for sharing their memories and photographs.

Thanks to Gareth Humphries MBE for spreading the word amongst my scouting friends, and to him, John Barnes, Andy Fisher, Brian Heeley, and Eddy and Margaret Worthington for sharing their scouting memories and photographs.

Thanks to Mrs Lang for sharing her Mere Oaks memories.

Thanks to Hunter Lodge and Wigan Council for kind permission to use their photographs.

Thanks to my Holly Road support workers for initially approaching Wigan Council about creating this book.

Thanks to Healthy Arts and Wigan Council for taking on this project, procuring funding for it and providing my co-writer Julie McKiernan, www.juleswriter.co.uk.

Thanks to Julie herself for her work on this book.

Thanks to the funders of this publication: City Health Care Partnership CIC, Newton-le-Willows Rotary Club, Hindley Rotary Club, and Taylor Wimpey Community Chest Initiative.

Thanks to CJ Harter for editing and proofreading the book, designing its interior, and seeing it through the publication process, www.cjharterbooks.co.uk/editingproofreading

Thanks to book cover designer Julian Watts, www.joolzdesign.com.

Lightning Source UK Ltd.
Milton Keynes UK
UKHW011503140620
364912UK00004B/1026